Contents

Words with lines underneath, like <u>this</u>, can be found in the glossary on page 24.

T0011975

Welcome

TO THE JUNGLE

Code monkeys are silly and smart. They want to learn all about computers and coding. You can follow the code monkeys and learn about coding too!

A code monkey's curiosity can get it into trouble. Hey! Don't eat that mouse!

CODE MONKEYS

Fix Bugs

BY JOHN WOOD

CRABTREE
PUBLISHING COMPANY
WWW.CRABTREEBOOKS.COM

CRABTREE
PUBLISHING COMPANY
WWW.CRABTREEBOOKS.COM

Author: John Wood

Editorial Director: Kathy Middleton

Editors: Madeline Tyler, Janine Deschenes

Proofreader: Melissa Boyce, Petrice Custance

Designed by: Danielle Webster-Jones

**Production coordinator and
 Prepress technician:** Margaret Amy Salter

Print coordinator: Katherine Berti

Images are courtesy of Shutterstock.com. With thanks to Getty Images, Thinkstock Photo and iStockphoto. Cover & throughout - Ori Artiste. 2 - Ann679. 4 - Ann679, GoodStudio, SK Design, feelplus. 5 - ppart. 6 - Robert Kneschke. 7 - Macrovector. 8-9 - Ann679, VectorKnight. 10 - Dean Drobot. 11 - l000s_pixels, PrinceOfLove. 12 - Kotofonya. 13 - Courtesy of the Naval Surface Warfare Center, Dahlgren, VA., 1988. [Public domain], Marish. 14 - Bakhtiar Zein. 15 - tynyuk. 17 - irin-k. 18 - Nadia Snopek. 19 - ajt. 22 - Ann679
Additional illustration by Danielle Webster-Jones.

Scratch is a project of the Scratch Foundation, in collaboration with the Lifelong Kindergarten Group at the MIT Media Lab. It is available for free at https://scratch.mit.edu

Library and Achives Canada Cataloguing in Publication

Title: Code monkeys fix bugs / by John Wood.
Other titles: Debugging
Names: Wood, John, 1990- author.
Series: Code monkeys.
Description: Series statement: Code Monkeys |
  Originally published under title: Debugging. King's Lynn: BookLife, 2020. |
  Includes index.
Identifiers: Canadiana (print) 20200222295 | Canadiana (ebook) 20200222430 |
  ISBN 9780778781493 (hardcover) |
  ISBN 9780778781530 (softcover) |
  ISBN 9781427125835 (HTML)
Subjects: LCSH: Debugging in computer science—Juvenile literature.
Classification: LCC QA76.9.D43 W66 2021 | DDC j005.1/4—dc23

Library of Congress Cataloging-in-Publication Data

Names: Wood, John, 1990- author.
Title: Code monkeys fix bugs / by John Wood.
Description: New York : Crabtree Publishing Company, 2021. |
  Series: Code monkeys | Includes index.
Identifiers: LCCN 2020016089 (print) | LCCN 2020016090 (ebook) |
  ISBN 9780778781493 (hardcover) |
  ISBN 9780778781530 (paperback) |
  ISBN 9781427125835 (ebook)
Subjects: LCSH: Debugging in computer science--Juvenile literature.
Classification: LCC QA76.9.D43 W66 2021 (print) |
  LCC QA76.9.D43 (ebook) | DDC 005.1/4--dc23
LC record available at https://lccn.loc.gov/2020016089
LC ebook record available at https://lccn.loc.gov/2020016090

Crabtree Publishing Company

www.crabtreebooks.com   1-800-387-7650

Published by Crabtree Publishing Company in 2021

Printed in the U.S.A./082020/CG20200601

**Published in Canada
Crabtree Publishing**
616 Welland Avenue
St. Catharines, Ontario
L2M 5V6

**Published in the United States
Crabtree Publishing**
347 Fifth Ave
Suite 1402-145
New York, NY 10016

SOME WORDS TO KNOW

COMPUTER

A machine that can carry out <u>instructions</u>.

CODING

Writing a set of instructions that tell computers what to do. The instructions are called code.

PROGRAMMER

A person who writes code, or puts instructions into a computer.

Computers are everywhere. Laptops, smartphones, desktops, and tablets are all computers. There are even computers in surprising places, from wristwatches to lampposts.

Coding
IN THE WILD

Applications, or apps, are <u>programs</u> used on computers. You might use one app to watch videos and another app to play games. Apps can also let you connect with others, create art, and learn in new ways.

Can you think of an app that helps you learn?

Every app is built out of code. If an app is not working as it should, a programmer needs to find what is wrong with the code. Finding and fixing coding mistakes is called debugging.

[ ]

</>

PHP

.com

Web

```
#[allow(unsafe_code)]
    unsafe extern "C" fn get_size
        (obj; *mut JSObject) -> usize{
    .....match get_dom_class(odj){
        .............oK(v)=>{
```

Some apps are built by big teams of programmers. Other apps are built by very few. Some programmers even create apps on their own.

WHAT ARE Bugs?

Silly monkeys! Stop looking for creepy, crawly bugs on the ground. In coding, a bug is a part of a code that doesn't work as it should.

Some bugs cause a program to <u>crash</u> and stop working. Other bugs might change how a program <u>behaves</u>. For example, a bug could cause a math program to give you the wrong answer when you add numbers. Or, a bug could erase your progress in an awesome game.

A bug could cause a program to make the same mistakes again and again.

WHAT CAUSES Bugs?

Computers cannot think for themselves the way humans can. They simply follow the instructions given to them. That means computers do not create bugs—programmers do!

Computers read code, not minds.

Bugs are often caused when a programmer makes a mistake when writing code. Code is the instructions given to a computer. Bugs happen when there is a problem with the instructions. Unclear instructions, spelling mistakes, and missing periods can all cause bugs.

Warning message

Error!

Cancel

FIND THOSE Bugs!

To fix bugs, programmers go through their code and look for mistakes. This process is called debugging. Sometimes, debugging takes a long time. Mistakes in code can be hard to find.

Debugging can be a difficult task!

Even the best programmers cannot write code perfectly every time. It is normal to make mistakes! Debugging is all about learning from mistakes. Debugging also teaches programmers how to solve problems!

LEARNING TO Debug

Here are some <u>common</u> bugs and mistakes in code. Programmers read the code step by step. They look carefully for these mistakes.

There might be a spelling mistake.

Instructions might be in the wrong order.

There might be missing instructions.

The instructions might be impossible for the computer to do.

Meet Baboolean. She is a robot monkey. The code monkeys have been writing code to make her complete certain tasks. They wrote code that tells Baboolean to take a bath. But she isn't completing the task correctly! Look closely at the code. Try reading it out loud. Can you find the bugs?

BATHTIME FOR BABOOLEAN

1. Appear next to bath
2. Turn taps off when bath is full
3. Turn taps on
4. Add bubbles
5. Add _____
6. Get in baff

BUGS

Step 1 will not work. Baboolean cannot just appear. Step 1 should read "Stand next to tub."

Step 2 is out of order. It should appear after "Add bubbles."

Step 5 has missing words (rubber duck).

Step 6 has a spelling mistake. "Baff" should be spelled "bath."

15

Testing
TIME

One way programmers look for bugs is by testing their code. They run the program again and again. They might get friends or other programmers to run the program too. Each time, they check to see if the program is doing anything wrong.

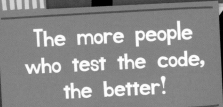

The more people who test the code, the better!

```
integer euclidAlgorithm (int A, int
B){
      A=Math.abs(A);
      B=Math.abs(B);
      while (B!=0){
            if (A>B) A=A-B;
            else B=B-A;
      }
      return A;
}

integer euclidAlgorithm (int A, int
B){
      A=Math.abs(A);
      B=Math.abs(B);
      while (B!=0){
            if (A>B) A=A-B;
            else B=B-A;
      }
      return A;
}

integer euclidAlgorithm (int A, int
B){
      A=Math.abs(A);
      B=Math.abs(B);
      while (B!=0){
            if (A>B) A=A-B;
            else B=B-A;
      }
      return A;
}
```

Many programmers create new games. They test their games by playing them again and again. People called playtesters play the games too. If something goes wrong or doesn't work as it should, they tell the programmer. Then, the programmer fixes the bugs.

Testing new games is called playtesting.

WRITING Clear Code

Finding bugs is easiest when we understand the code we read.
So programmers try to write code in a way that is neat and clear.
They try to write short and simple instructions to make code easy to read.

It would be hard to find a bug in messy code!

Leaving comments is another way programmers make code easy to understand. The comments let others know how the code should work. These comments are not read by the computer.

```
# This code makes Baboolean say
"ooh ooh ah ah" five times.

for loop in range (5):
    print ("ooh ooh ah ah")
```

Computers know not to read the comments because the programmer marks them with <u>symbols</u> such as # or //. Different <u>programming languages</u> use different symbols.

"ooh ooh ah ah
ooh ooh ah ah
ooh ooh ah ah
ooh ooh ah ah
ooh ooh ah ah"

Monkey See

The code monkeys have been working hard to learn how to code. Here are some lines of code they have been writing. Oh dear! Look at all of the bugs.

This monkey has been coding in a programming language called <u>JavaScript</u>. In JavaScript, any opening <u>brackets</u> need to have closing brackets too. Brackets in JavaScript could look like this: ( ), [ ], { }. But this monkey has forgotten to put closing brackets here! This code will not work.

```
<!DOCTYPE html>
<html>
<head>
        <title> Food Fight </title>
<script>
function foodFight() {
        var monkeys = 6
        var bananas = 5;
        if (monkeys > bananas      { alert("Food Fight!"); } }
foodFight();
</script>
</head>
</html>
```

Don't worry if this looks <u>complicated</u>! All you need to know is that code can't have a single mistake in it, no matter how small, or it will not work properly.

Monkey Do

Look at these two sets of instructions for Baboolean. Can you see any bugs? The answers are on page 23.

HOW TO HANG FROM A TREE BRANCH

Z: Climb tree
2: Take your hands and feet off the branch
3: Wrap tail around a strong branch
4: Hang upside down by tayul

HOW TO CLEAN YOUR MONKEY FRIEND

1: Find a monkey friend

2: Look for creepy crawly bug in monkey friend's fur

3: Sit next to monkey friend

4: Grab creepy crawly bug with ears

5: Put creepy crawly bug ▨▨▨▨▨ and chew

6: Swallow creepy crawly bug

7: Burp

in mouth

Answers

HOW TO HANG FROM A TREE BRANCH

> 2 should be a 1
> Switch Steps 2 and 3
> Tail is spelled wrong in Step 4

HOW TO CLEAN YOUR MONKEY FRIEND

> Switch Steps 2 and 3
> Steps 4 is impossible. Change "ears" to "fingers."
> In Step 5, the words "in mouth" are missing

23

Glossary

behaves How something or someone acts or functions

brackets A pair of marks that group words, numbers, or symbols together

common Describes something that happens regularly or often

complicated Made of many different parts and difficult to understand

computer scientist A person who studies how computers are made and how they work

crash In computers, when a program stops working and closes

instructions A set of steps that explain how something is done

JavaScript A type of programming language that is good for building websites that are interactive, or involve communication between the user and computer

programming languages Languages that humans use to write instructions for computers.

programs Collections of instructions that let computers complete certain tasks

Scratch A type of programming language made up of blocks. Scratch is a good programming language for beginner coders.

symbols Objects or pictures that represent, or stand for, something else

Index